Automate Your Office

Practical Tips and Tools to Enhance Productivity

Joseph Simon

Automate Your Office

TABLE OF CONTENTS

Chapter 1: Understanding Office Automation

What is Office Automation?

Office automation represents a transformative shift in how businesses operate, streamlining processes and enhancing productivity through the integration of technology. At its core, office automation involves the use of various software and hardware solutions to perform routine tasks that were traditionally handled manually. This evolution has not only redefined the workplace but also empowered organizations to focus on strategic initiatives by reducing the time and effort spent on mundane activities.

The concept of office automation is not new; it has been evolving for decades. Initially, it began with the introduction of basic tools like typewriters and calculators, which simplified clerical work. As technology advanced, so did the capabilities of office automation. The advent of personal computers in the late 20th century marked a significant milestone, enabling the digitization of documents and the automation of data processing tasks. This laid the groundwork for the sophisticated systems we see today, which encompass everything from email management to complex data analytics.

One of the primary benefits of office automation is the increased efficiency it brings to an organization. By automating repetitive tasks, employees can allocate their time and energy to more value-added activities. For instance, automated scheduling tools can manage appointments and meetings without the need for constant human intervention, freeing up administrative staff to focus on more critical responsibilities. Similarly, document management systems can organize, store, and retrieve files with ease, reducing the time spent searching for information.

Cost savings are another significant advantage of office automation. By minimizing manual labor and reducing errors, businesses can lower operational expenses. Automated systems often require less manpower to maintain, allowing companies to optimize their workforce and allocate resources more effectively. Additionally, automation can lead to faster turnaround times, improving customer satisfaction and potentially increasing revenue.

Despite its numerous advantages, office automation is often misunderstood. A common misconception is that automation leads to job loss, as machines replace human workers. While it's true that automation can change the nature of certain roles, it also creates new opportunities for employees to engage in more meaningful work. By taking over routine tasks, automation allows individuals to develop new skills and take on more strategic roles within the organization. Moreover, the demand for professionals who can manage and maintain automated systems is on the rise, creating a new job market.

Another misconception is that office automation is only suitable for large corporations with substantial budgets. In reality, automation solutions are scalable and can be tailored to fit the needs of businesses of all sizes. Small and medium-sized enterprises can benefit from automation just as much as their larger counterparts, often gaining a competitive edge by adopting these technologies early. Cloud-based solutions, in particular, offer affordable and flexible options for businesses looking to automate their operations without significant upfront investment.

The future of office automation is promising, with emerging technologies poised to further revolutionize the workplace. Artificial intelligence and machine learning are at the forefront of this evolution, enabling systems to learn from data and make intelligent decisions. These technologies can enhance automation by predicting trends, optimizing processes, and providing insights that were previously unattainable. For example, AI-powered chatbots can handle customer inquiries with increasing sophistication, offering personalized responses and improving the overall customer experience.

Robotic process automation (RPA) is another area of growth, allowing businesses to automate complex workflows that involve multiple systems and applications. RPA can mimic human actions, such as data entry and transaction processing, with greater speed and accuracy. This technology is particularly beneficial for industries with high volumes of repetitive tasks, such as finance and healthcare, where precision and efficiency are paramount.

As office automation continues to evolve, organizations must remain adaptable and open to change. Embracing automation requires a cultural shift, where employees are encouraged to view technology as an enabler rather than a threat. Training and development programs can help staff acquire the skills needed to thrive in an automated environment, ensuring a smooth transition and maximizing the benefits of automation.

In conclusion, office automation is a powerful tool that can transform the way businesses operate, offering increased efficiency, cost savings, and new opportunities for growth. By understanding its potential and addressing common misconceptions, organizations can harness the power of automation to drive innovation and achieve their strategic objectives. As technology continues to advance, the possibilities for office automation are limitless, promising a future where businesses can operate with unprecedented agility and effectiveness.

Historical Development of Automation Tools

The journey of automation tools in the office environment is a fascinating tale of innovation and adaptation, reflecting broader technological advancements and shifts in workplace culture. The roots of office automation can be traced back to the late 19th and early 20th centuries, a period marked by the industrial revolution and the burgeoning need for efficiency in business operations. During this era, the introduction of mechanical devices such as typewriters and adding machines began to transform the way clerical work was performed. These early tools laid the groundwork for the more sophisticated systems that would follow, setting the stage for a revolution in office productivity.

The typewriter, patented in the 1860s, was one of the first significant breakthroughs in office automation. It revolutionized the way documents were produced, offering a faster and more legible alternative to handwritten text. The typewriter became an indispensable tool in offices worldwide, symbolizing the shift towards mechanization in administrative tasks. Alongside the typewriter, the invention of the telephone in the late 19th century transformed communication, allowing for real-time interaction over long distances and facilitating more efficient business operations.

As the 20th century progressed, the development of electronic devices further accelerated the pace of office automation. The introduction of the photocopier in the 1950s, for instance, revolutionized document reproduction, enabling businesses to quickly and easily duplicate important papers. This innovation not only saved time but also reduced the costs associated with manual copying, making it a staple in offices around the globe.

The advent of computers in the latter half of the 20th century marked a pivotal moment in the history of office automation. Initially, computers were large, expensive machines accessible only to large corporations and government agencies. However, the development of the personal computer in the 1980s democratized access to computing power, bringing it into the hands of small businesses and individual users. This shift had a profound impact on office automation, as computers could perform a wide range of tasks, from word processing to complex data analysis, with unprecedented speed and accuracy.

Software development played a crucial role in the evolution of office automation during this period. The creation of word processing programs, spreadsheets, and database management systems transformed the way information was handled and processed. These tools enabled businesses to automate routine tasks, such as document creation and data entry, freeing up employees to focus on more strategic activities. The rise of the internet in the 1990s further expanded the possibilities for office automation, facilitating communication and collaboration on a global scale.

Email, one of the most significant innovations of the internet era, revolutionized business communication by providing a fast, efficient, and cost-effective means of exchanging information.

The ability to send and receive messages instantly transformed the way organizations operated, reducing the reliance on traditional mail and enabling more agile decision-making processes. As email became ubiquitous, it paved the way for the development of other digital communication tools, such as instant messaging and video conferencing, which further enhanced collaboration and connectivity in the workplace.

The turn of the 21st century saw the emergence of cloud computing, a technology that has had a profound impact on office automation. By allowing businesses to store and access data and applications over the internet, cloud computing has enabled greater flexibility and scalability in office operations. Organizations can now deploy automation tools without the need for significant upfront investment in hardware and infrastructure, making it accessible to businesses of all sizes. Cloud-based solutions also facilitate remote work and collaboration, breaking down geographical barriers and enabling teams to work together seamlessly, regardless of location.

In recent years, the development of mobile technology has further transformed office automation, enabling employees to access tools and information from anywhere, at any time. Smartphones and tablets have become essential components of the modern workplace, allowing for greater mobility and flexibility in how work is conducted. Mobile apps for project management, communication, and document editing have become integral to office automation, empowering employees to stay connected and productive on the go.

The historical development of automation tools in the office environment is a testament to the relentless pursuit of efficiency and productivity. From the mechanical devices of the industrial revolution to the digital innovations of the 21st century, each advancement has built upon the last, creating a rich tapestry of technological progress. As we look to the future, the continued evolution of automation tools promises to further transform the workplace, offering new opportunities for innovation and growth. The journey of office automation is far from over, and the possibilities for what lies ahead are limited only by our imagination.

Benefits of Office Automation

Office automation has become an integral part of modern business operations, offering a multitude of benefits that enhance productivity, efficiency, and overall workplace satisfaction. As organizations strive to remain competitive in an ever-evolving market, the adoption of automation tools has proven to be a strategic advantage. By streamlining routine tasks and optimizing workflows, office automation empowers employees to focus on more value-added activities, ultimately driving business success.

One of the most significant benefits of office automation is the increase in productivity it affords. By automating repetitive and time-consuming tasks, such as data entry, scheduling, and document management, employees can devote more time to strategic initiatives and creative problem-solving. This shift not only enhances individual performance but also contributes to the overall efficiency of the organization. Automation tools can process large volumes of information quickly and accurately, reducing the likelihood of human error and ensuring that tasks are completed in a timely manner.

In addition to boosting productivity, office automation also improves communication and collaboration within organizations. Digital communication tools, such as email, instant messaging, and video conferencing, facilitate seamless interaction among team members, regardless of their physical location. This connectivity fosters a more collaborative work environment, enabling employees to share ideas, provide feedback, and work together on projects with ease. The ability to communicate and collaborate effectively is particularly valuable in today's globalized business landscape, where remote work and virtual teams are becoming increasingly common.

Another key advantage of office automation is the enhancement of data management and accessibility. Automation tools enable organizations to store, organize, and retrieve information efficiently, ensuring that employees have access to the data they need when they need it. This capability is particularly important in industries that rely heavily on data-driven decision-making, such as finance, healthcare, and marketing. By providing real-time access to accurate and up-to-date information, office automation supports informed decision-making and strategic planning.

Cost savings are another compelling benefit of office automation. By reducing the need for manual labor and minimizing the risk of errors, automation tools can significantly lower operational costs. For example, automated billing and invoicing systems can streamline financial processes, reducing the time and resources required to manage accounts payable and receivable. Similarly, automated inventory management systems can optimize stock levels, minimizing waste and ensuring that resources are allocated efficiently. These cost savings can be reinvested in other areas of the business, such as research and development or employee training, further contributing to organizational growth and success.

Office automation also plays a crucial role in enhancing customer service and satisfaction. By automating routine customer interactions, such as order processing and support inquiries, organizations can provide faster and more consistent service. Automation tools can handle high volumes of customer requests simultaneously, ensuring that inquiries are addressed promptly and accurately. This efficiency not only improves the customer experience but also frees up employees to focus on more complex and personalized interactions, further strengthening customer relationships.

The implementation of office automation can also lead to improved employee satisfaction and engagement. By alleviating the burden of mundane and repetitive tasks, automation allows employees to focus on more meaningful and fulfilling work. This shift can lead to increased job satisfaction, as employees are able to leverage their skills and expertise in more impactful ways. Additionally, the use of automation tools can provide employees with greater flexibility and autonomy in how they manage their work, contributing to a more positive and empowering work environment.

Furthermore, office automation can enhance organizational agility and adaptability. In a rapidly changing business landscape, the ability to respond quickly to new opportunities and challenges is critical. Automation tools enable organizations to streamline processes and workflows, allowing them to pivot and adapt with ease. This agility is particularly valuable in industries characterized by frequent technological advancements and shifting consumer demands, where staying ahead of the curve is essential for success.

The environmental benefits of office automation should not be overlooked. By reducing the reliance on paper-based processes and minimizing waste, automation tools contribute to more sustainable business practices. Digital document management systems, for example, eliminate the need for physical storage and printing, reducing the organization's carbon footprint. Additionally, automation can optimize resource allocation and energy consumption, further supporting environmental sustainability efforts.

The benefits of office automation are manifold, offering organizations a strategic advantage in today's competitive business environment. By enhancing productivity, communication, data management, and customer service, automation tools empower organizations to operate more efficiently and effectively. The cost savings, employee satisfaction, and environmental sustainability associated with automation further underscore its value as a critical component of modern business operations. As technology continues to evolve, the potential for office automation to drive innovation and growth will only continue to expand, offering exciting possibilities for the future of work.

Common Misconceptions

Misconceptions often cloud our understanding, leading us astray from the truth. In the realm of office automation, these misconceptions can hinder progress and prevent organizations from fully embracing the benefits that automation offers. By addressing these misunderstandings, we can pave the way for a more informed and effective adoption of automation technologies.

One prevalent misconception is that office automation will lead to widespread job loss. This fear stems from the belief that machines will replace human workers, rendering their roles obsolete. However, the reality is more nuanced. While automation does streamline certain tasks, it also creates new opportunities for employees to engage in more meaningful and strategic work. By automating repetitive and mundane tasks, employees can focus on activities that require creativity, critical thinking, and problem-solving skills. This shift not only enhances job satisfaction but also contributes to the overall growth and innovation of the organization.

Another common misconception is that office automation is only suitable for large corporations with substantial resources. Many small and medium-sized enterprises (SMEs) believe that automation is beyond their reach, both financially and logistically. However, advancements in technology have made automation tools more accessible and affordable than ever before. Cloud-based solutions, for example, offer scalable and cost-effective options for businesses of all sizes. By leveraging these tools, SMEs can enhance their efficiency and competitiveness without incurring prohibitive costs.

Some individuals mistakenly believe that office automation is a one-size-fits-all solution. They assume that implementing automation tools will automatically resolve all operational challenges. In reality, successful automation requires a tailored approach that considers the unique needs and goals of each organization. It is essential to conduct a thorough assessment of existing processes and identify areas where automation can provide the most value. By customizing automation solutions to align with specific business objectives, organizations can maximize the benefits and achieve sustainable improvements.

There is also a misconception that office automation is solely about technology. While technology plays a crucial role, the human element is equally important. Successful automation requires a cultural shift within the organization, where employees are encouraged to embrace change and adopt new ways of working. This shift involves fostering a mindset of continuous learning and adaptation, where employees are empowered to leverage automation tools to enhance their productivity and effectiveness. By prioritizing both technology and people, organizations can create a harmonious and dynamic work environment.

Some individuals fear that automation will lead to a loss of control over business processes. They worry that relying on automated systems will result in a lack of oversight and accountability. However, automation can actually enhance control and transparency by providing real-time data and insights into operations. Automation tools can track and monitor processes with precision, ensuring that tasks are completed accurately and efficiently. This level of visibility enables organizations to make informed decisions and maintain a high standard of quality and compliance.

Another misconception is that office automation is a complex and time-consuming endeavor. Some organizations hesitate to adopt automation tools due to concerns about the implementation process and potential disruptions to daily operations. While it is true that automation requires careful planning and execution, the long-term benefits far outweigh the initial investment. By partnering with experienced vendors and leveraging user-friendly solutions, organizations can streamline the implementation process and minimize disruptions. Additionally, many automation tools offer intuitive interfaces and comprehensive support, making it easier for employees to adapt and integrate them into their workflows.

There is a belief that automation stifles creativity and innovation. Some individuals fear that by relying on automated systems, organizations will lose the human touch and the ability to think outside the box. However, automation can actually foster creativity by freeing up time and resources for employees to explore new ideas and approaches. By automating routine tasks, employees can focus on strategic initiatives and innovative projects that drive business growth. Automation can also facilitate collaboration and knowledge sharing, enabling teams to work together more effectively and generate fresh insights.

A common misconception is that automation is a static solution that requires little maintenance or updates. In reality, automation is an evolving process that requires ongoing evaluation and optimization. As business needs and technologies change, organizations must continuously assess their automation strategies and make necessary adjustments. This iterative approach ensures that automation remains aligned with organizational goals and continues to deliver value over time. By embracing a mindset of continuous improvement, organizations can stay ahead of the curve and capitalize on emerging opportunities.

Some individuals mistakenly believe that automation is only relevant to certain industries or functions. They assume that automation is limited to manufacturing or IT-related tasks.

However, automation has applications across a wide range of industries and functions, from finance and healthcare to marketing and customer service. By exploring the diverse possibilities of automation, organizations can identify areas where it can enhance efficiency, accuracy, and customer satisfaction. This broad applicability makes automation a versatile and valuable tool for businesses of all types and sizes.

Misconceptions about office automation can create barriers to its successful adoption and implementation. By addressing these misunderstandings and providing accurate information, organizations can make informed decisions and fully leverage the benefits of automation. Embracing automation with an open mind and a strategic approach can lead to transformative outcomes, empowering organizations to thrive in an increasingly competitive and dynamic business landscape.

Future Trends in Office Automation

The landscape of office automation is rapidly evolving, driven by technological advancements and changing workplace dynamics. As organizations strive to enhance efficiency and productivity, understanding future trends in office automation becomes crucial. These trends not only shape the way businesses operate but also redefine the roles of employees and the nature of work itself.

One significant trend is the increasing integration of automation with cloud computing. Cloud-based solutions offer scalability, flexibility, and accessibility, making them an ideal platform for automation tools. By leveraging the cloud, organizations can streamline processes, reduce infrastructure costs, and enable remote work. This trend is particularly relevant in the context of the growing demand for hybrid work models, where employees split their time between the office and remote locations. Cloud-based automation ensures seamless collaboration and data sharing, regardless of geographical boundaries.

Another emerging trend is the rise of intelligent automation, which combines traditional automation with advanced technologies such as machine learning and natural language processing. Intelligent automation enables systems to learn from data, adapt to changing conditions, and make informed decisions. This capability enhances the efficiency and accuracy of automated processes, allowing organizations to handle complex tasks with minimal human intervention. As intelligent automation continues to evolve, it is expected to play a pivotal role in areas such as customer service, data analysis, and supply chain management.

The growing emphasis on data-driven decision-making is also shaping the future of office automation. Organizations are increasingly relying on data analytics to gain insights and drive strategic initiatives. Automation tools equipped with data analytics capabilities can process vast amounts of information, identify patterns, and generate actionable insights. This trend empowers businesses to make informed decisions, optimize operations, and anticipate market trends. As data becomes a critical asset, the integration of analytics into automation solutions will become a standard practice.

The trend towards personalization is gaining momentum in office automation. Organizations are recognizing the importance of tailoring automation solutions to meet the unique needs and preferences of individual users. Personalized automation enhances user experience, increases adoption rates, and boosts productivity. For example, customizable dashboards and interfaces allow employees to access relevant information and tools quickly. This trend reflects a broader shift towards user-centric design, where technology adapts to the user rather than the other way around.

Sustainability is becoming a key consideration in the development of office automation solutions. As environmental concerns continue to rise, organizations are seeking ways to reduce their carbon footprint and promote sustainable practices. Automation can contribute to sustainability by optimizing resource usage, minimizing waste, and reducing energy consumption. For instance, automated systems can monitor and control energy usage in office buildings, leading to significant cost savings and environmental benefits. The integration of sustainability into automation strategies aligns with the growing demand for corporate social responsibility and ethical business practices.

The trend of increased collaboration between humans and machines is reshaping the workplace. Rather than replacing human workers, automation is augmenting their capabilities and enabling them to focus on higher-value tasks. Collaborative automation tools facilitate seamless interaction between humans and machines, allowing employees to leverage technology to enhance their performance. This trend underscores the importance of reskilling and upskilling the workforce to adapt to new roles and responsibilities. Organizations that invest in training and development will be better positioned to harness the full potential of automation.

Security and privacy concerns are becoming more prominent as office automation becomes more pervasive. With the increasing reliance on digital systems and data, organizations must prioritize cybersecurity measures to protect sensitive information and maintain trust. Automation solutions must incorporate robust security features to safeguard against cyber threats and data breaches. Additionally, organizations must establish clear policies and protocols to ensure compliance with data protection regulations. As security challenges evolve, the focus on cybersecurity in office automation will continue to intensify.

The trend towards seamless integration of automation tools with existing systems is gaining traction. Organizations are seeking solutions that can easily integrate with their current infrastructure and workflows. This trend reflects the need for interoperability and compatibility, allowing businesses to maximize the value of their technology investments. Seamless integration ensures that automation tools work harmoniously with other systems, reducing disruptions and enhancing overall efficiency. As organizations strive for digital transformation, the demand for integrated automation solutions will continue to grow.

The future of office automation is also characterized by the democratization of technology. Automation tools are becoming more accessible to a wider range of users, regardless of their technical expertise. User-friendly interfaces, low-code platforms, and intuitive design are making it easier for employees to adopt and utilize automation solutions. This trend empowers individuals across the organization to contribute to process improvement and innovation. By democratizing technology, organizations can foster a culture of collaboration and continuous improvement.

The evolution of office automation is closely linked to the changing nature of work. As organizations embrace flexible work arrangements and prioritize employee well-being, automation will play a crucial role in supporting these initiatives. Automation can enhance work-life balance by reducing the burden of repetitive tasks and enabling employees to focus on meaningful work. Additionally, automation can facilitate remote work by providing the necessary tools and infrastructure for virtual collaboration. As the future of work continues to evolve, office automation will remain a key enabler of productivity and innovation.

Understanding future trends in office automation is essential for organizations seeking to stay competitive and agile in a rapidly changing business environment. By embracing these trends, businesses can unlock new opportunities, drive efficiency, and create a more dynamic and resilient workplace. As technology continues to advance, the potential of office automation will only grow, offering exciting possibilities for the future of work.

Chapter 2: Assessing Your Current Workflow

Workflow Analysis Techniques

Understanding workflow analysis techniques is essential for optimizing business processes and enhancing productivity. By examining the flow of tasks and identifying inefficiencies, organizations can streamline operations and improve overall performance. This chapter delves into various techniques that can be employed to analyze workflows effectively, providing practical insights for beginners seeking to enhance their understanding of this critical aspect of business management.

One fundamental technique in workflow analysis is process mapping. This involves creating a visual representation of a workflow, detailing each step and the sequence in which tasks are performed. Process maps can take various forms, such as flowcharts, swimlane diagrams, or value stream maps. These visual tools help identify bottlenecks, redundancies, and areas for improvement. By mapping out a process, organizations can gain a clearer understanding of how work is currently being done and where changes can be made to enhance efficiency.

Another valuable technique is time-motion study, which focuses on measuring the time taken to complete each task within a workflow. By analyzing the time spent on different activities, organizations can identify tasks that consume excessive time and resources. This technique is particularly useful for identifying areas where automation or process reengineering can lead to significant time savings. Time-motion studies provide a quantitative basis for decision-making, enabling organizations to prioritize improvements based on their potential impact on productivity.

Root cause analysis is a technique used to identify the underlying causes of workflow inefficiencies. By examining the root causes of problems, organizations can develop targeted solutions that address the source of the issue rather than just its symptoms. Techniques such as the "5 Whys" or fishbone diagrams can be employed to systematically explore the factors contributing to workflow challenges. Root cause analysis helps organizations implement sustainable improvements that prevent recurring issues and enhance overall process performance.

Benchmarking is another technique that can be employed to analyze workflows. This involves comparing an organization's processes with those of industry leaders or best-in-class organizations. By identifying gaps between current performance and industry standards, organizations can set realistic improvement targets and adopt best practices. Benchmarking provides valuable insights into how similar organizations achieve high levels of efficiency and effectiveness, offering a roadmap for enhancing one's own workflows.

Value-added analysis is a technique that focuses on distinguishing between value-added and non-value-added activities within a workflow. Value-added activities are those that directly contribute to meeting customer needs or achieving organizational goals, while non-value-added activities do not add value and may even hinder performance. By identifying and eliminating non-value-added activities, organizations can streamline workflows and enhance overall efficiency. This technique encourages a customer-centric approach to process improvement, ensuring that resources are allocated to activities that truly matter.

Simulation modeling is a powerful technique that allows organizations to test different scenarios and assess the impact of changes on workflow performance. By creating a virtual model of a workflow, organizations can experiment with various process configurations and evaluate their effects on key performance indicators. Simulation modeling provides a risk-free environment for testing process improvements, enabling organizations to make informed decisions before implementing changes in the real world. This technique is particularly valuable for complex workflows with multiple interdependencies.

The use of data analytics in workflow analysis is becoming increasingly prevalent. By leveraging data analytics tools, organizations can gain insights into workflow performance, identify patterns, and predict future trends. Data analytics enables organizations to make data-driven decisions, optimize resource allocation, and enhance process efficiency. Techniques such as process mining can be used to extract valuable information from event logs, providing a detailed view of how workflows are executed in practice. Data analytics empowers organizations to continuously monitor and improve workflows based on real-time data.

Employee feedback is an often-overlooked technique in workflow analysis. Employees who are directly involved in executing workflows possess valuable insights into the challenges and opportunities for improvement. By soliciting feedback from employees, organizations can gain a deeper understanding of workflow dynamics and identify practical solutions. Techniques such as surveys, interviews, or focus groups can be used to gather employee input and foster a culture of continuous improvement. Employee feedback ensures that workflow analysis is grounded in the realities of day-to-day operations.

The integration of technology into workflow analysis is transforming the way organizations approach process improvement. Advanced tools and software solutions enable organizations to automate data collection, visualize workflows, and track performance metrics. Technology facilitates real-time monitoring and analysis, allowing organizations to respond quickly to changing conditions and emerging opportunities. By harnessing the power of technology, organizations can enhance the accuracy and efficiency of workflow analysis, driving more effective decision-making and process optimization.

Understanding and applying workflow analysis techniques is essential for organizations seeking to enhance efficiency and competitiveness. By employing techniques such as process mapping, time-motion study, root cause analysis, benchmarking, value-added analysis, simulation modeling, data analytics, employee feedback, and technology integration, organizations can gain valuable insights into their workflows and implement targeted improvements. These techniques provide a comprehensive toolkit for analyzing and optimizing workflows, enabling organizations to achieve higher levels of performance and success.

Identifying Bottlenecks and Inefficiencies

Identifying bottlenecks and inefficiencies within a workflow is a crucial step in optimizing business processes and enhancing productivity. These obstacles can significantly hinder an organization's ability to achieve its goals, leading to delays, increased costs, and reduced customer satisfaction. By pinpointing these issues, businesses can implement targeted solutions to streamline operations and improve overall performance.

One effective method for identifying bottlenecks is through process observation. This involves closely monitoring the workflow as it unfolds, paying attention to areas where tasks slow down or come to a halt. Observing the process in real-time allows for the identification of specific points where work accumulates, leading to delays. This hands-on approach provides valuable insights into the practical challenges faced by employees and highlights areas where improvements can be made.

Another technique is the use of process mapping, which involves creating a visual representation of the workflow. By mapping out each step and the sequence in which tasks are performed, organizations can gain a clearer understanding of how work is currently being done. Process maps, such as flowcharts or swimlane diagrams, help identify redundancies, unnecessary steps, and areas where tasks overlap. This visual tool serves as a foundation for analyzing the workflow and pinpointing inefficiencies that may not be immediately apparent.

Data analysis plays a significant role in identifying bottlenecks and inefficiencies. By collecting and analyzing data related to workflow performance, organizations can uncover patterns and trends that indicate problem areas. Key performance indicators (KPIs) such as cycle time, lead time, and throughput can be used to measure the efficiency of a process. By comparing these metrics against industry benchmarks or historical data, organizations can identify deviations that signal potential bottlenecks. Data analysis provides a quantitative basis for decision-making, enabling organizations to prioritize improvements based on their impact on performance.

Employee feedback is an invaluable resource for identifying bottlenecks and inefficiencies. Employees who are directly involved in executing workflows possess firsthand knowledge of the challenges and obstacles they encounter. By soliciting feedback through surveys, interviews, or focus groups, organizations can gain insights into the practical realities of the workflow. Employees may offer suggestions for improvement or highlight specific areas where they experience delays or frustration. This collaborative approach fosters a culture of continuous improvement and ensures that solutions are grounded in the realities of day-to-day operations.

Root cause analysis is a technique used to identify the underlying causes of bottlenecks and inefficiencies. By examining the root causes of problems, organizations can develop targeted solutions that address the source of the issue rather than just its symptoms. Techniques such as the "5 Whys" or fishbone diagrams can be employed to systematically explore the factors contributing to workflow challenges. Root cause analysis helps organizations implement sustainable improvements that prevent recurring issues and enhance overall process performance.

Simulation modeling is a powerful tool for identifying bottlenecks and inefficiencies in complex workflows. By creating a virtual model of the workflow, organizations can experiment with different scenarios and assess the impact of changes on performance. Simulation modeling allows for the testing of various process configurations, enabling organizations to identify potential bottlenecks before they occur in the real world. This technique provides a risk-free environment for exploring process improvements and making informed decisions.

Benchmarking is another technique that can be employed to identify bottlenecks and inefficiencies. By comparing an organization's processes with those of industry leaders or best-in-class organizations, businesses can identify gaps between current performance and industry standards. Benchmarking provides valuable insights into how similar organizations achieve high levels of efficiency and effectiveness, offering a roadmap for enhancing one's own workflows. By adopting best practices and setting realistic improvement targets, organizations can address bottlenecks and inefficiencies more effectively.

The integration of technology into workflow analysis is transforming the way organizations identify and address bottlenecks and inefficiencies. Advanced tools and software solutions enable organizations to automate data collection, visualize workflows, and track performance metrics. Technology facilitates real-time monitoring and analysis, allowing organizations to respond quickly to changing conditions and emerging opportunities. By harnessing the power of technology, organizations can enhance the accuracy and efficiency of workflow analysis, driving more effective decision-making and process optimization.

Understanding and addressing bottlenecks and inefficiencies is essential for organizations seeking to enhance efficiency and competitiveness. By employing techniques such as process observation, process mapping, data analysis, employee feedback, root cause analysis, simulation modeling, benchmarking, and technology integration, organizations can gain valuable insights into their workflows and implement targeted improvements. These techniques provide a comprehensive toolkit for analyzing and optimizing workflows, enabling organizations to achieve higher levels of performance and success.

Setting Priorities for Automation

Setting priorities for automation is a critical step in optimizing business processes and enhancing efficiency. With the rapid advancement of technology, organizations are increasingly turning to automation to streamline operations, reduce costs, and improve productivity. However, not all processes are equally suited for automation, and identifying which tasks to prioritize requires careful consideration and strategic planning.

The first step in setting priorities for automation is to conduct a thorough assessment of existing workflows. This involves analyzing each process to determine its complexity, frequency, and impact on overall business objectives. Processes that are repetitive, time-consuming, and prone to human error are often prime candidates for automation. By focusing on these tasks, organizations can achieve significant time savings and reduce the likelihood of costly mistakes.

Once potential processes for automation have been identified, it's important to evaluate the potential return on investment (ROI) for each. This involves considering the costs associated with implementing automation solutions, such as software, hardware, and training, against the anticipated benefits. These benefits may include increased efficiency, reduced labor costs, and improved accuracy. By calculating the ROI, organizations can prioritize processes that offer the greatest potential for cost savings and performance improvements.

Another key factor to consider when setting priorities for automation is the impact on employees. Automation can lead to changes in job roles and responsibilities, and it's important to ensure that employees are prepared for these changes. Engaging employees in the decision-making process and providing training and support can help ease the transition and foster a positive attitude towards automation. By considering the human element, organizations can ensure that automation initiatives are successful and sustainable.

In addition to assessing individual processes, it's important to consider the broader organizational context when setting priorities for automation. This involves aligning automation initiatives with strategic business goals and objectives. For example, if an organization is focused on improving customer service, automating processes that directly impact customer interactions, such as order processing or customer support, may be a priority. By aligning automation efforts with business goals, organizations can ensure that they are making the most effective use of their resources.

Risk assessment is another important consideration when setting priorities for automation. Some processes may be more critical to business operations than others, and automating these tasks may carry a higher level of risk. It's important to carefully evaluate the potential risks associated with automation, such as system failures or data breaches, and implement appropriate safeguards. By conducting a thorough risk assessment, organizations can prioritize processes that offer the greatest benefits while minimizing potential risks.

Once priorities have been established, it's important to develop a clear implementation plan for automation. This involves setting specific goals and timelines, allocating resources, and identifying key stakeholders. A well-defined plan ensures that automation initiatives are executed efficiently and effectively, with minimal disruption to business operations. Regular monitoring and evaluation of automation efforts are also essential to ensure that they continue to deliver the desired results.

Collaboration and communication are key to the success of automation initiatives. Engaging stakeholders from across the organization, including IT, operations, and management, ensures that all perspectives are considered and that automation efforts are aligned with organizational needs. Regular communication and feedback loops help identify potential issues early on and ensure that automation initiatives remain on track.

Technology selection is a critical component of setting priorities for automation. With a wide range of automation solutions available, it's important to choose the right tools for the job. This involves evaluating different technologies based on their capabilities, scalability, and compatibility with existing systems. By selecting the most appropriate technology, organizations can ensure that their automation efforts are effective and sustainable.

Continuous improvement is an essential aspect of successful automation. As technology evolves and business needs change, it's important to regularly review and update automation initiatives. This involves monitoring performance metrics, gathering feedback from employees and stakeholders, and making adjustments as needed. By fostering a culture of continuous improvement, organizations can ensure that their automation efforts remain relevant and effective over time.

Setting priorities for automation is a complex and multifaceted process that requires careful consideration and strategic planning. By conducting a thorough assessment of existing workflows, evaluating potential ROI, considering the impact on employees, aligning with business goals, assessing risks, developing a clear implementation plan, fostering collaboration and communication, selecting the right technology, and embracing continuous improvement, organizations can successfully prioritize and implement automation initiatives that drive efficiency and enhance performance.

Creating an Automation Roadmap

Creating an automation roadmap is a strategic endeavor that requires careful planning and foresight. It serves as a blueprint for organizations aiming to integrate automation into their operations, ensuring that the transition is smooth, efficient, and aligned with broader business objectives. The roadmap not only outlines the steps necessary for implementation but also helps in anticipating challenges and measuring success.

The journey begins with a clear understanding of the organization's current state. This involves conducting a comprehensive audit of existing processes, systems, and technologies. By mapping out the current landscape, organizations can identify areas where automation can have the most significant impact. This initial assessment should consider factors such as process complexity, frequency, and the potential for error reduction. Engaging with employees who are directly involved in these processes can provide valuable insights and help in identifying pain points that automation could alleviate.

Once the current state is well-documented, the next step is to define the desired future state. This involves setting clear, achievable goals for what the organization hopes to accomplish through automation. These goals should be aligned with the organization's overall strategic objectives, whether they involve improving efficiency, reducing costs, enhancing customer service, or driving innovation. By establishing a clear vision of the future state, organizations can ensure that their automation efforts are purposeful and targeted.

With a clear understanding of both the current and future states, the next phase involves identifying specific processes for automation. This requires a careful evaluation of each process to determine its suitability for automation. Processes that are repetitive, time-consuming, and prone to human error are often ideal candidates. However, it's also important to consider the potential impact on employees and the organization as a whole. Engaging stakeholders from across the organization can help ensure that all perspectives are considered and that the selected processes align with broader business goals.

After identifying the processes to be automated, the next step is to prioritize them. Not all processes can be automated simultaneously, and prioritization is essential to ensure that resources are allocated effectively. This involves evaluating each process based on factors such as potential ROI, impact on business objectives, and ease of implementation. By prioritizing processes, organizations can focus their efforts on areas that offer the greatest potential benefits.

With priorities established, the roadmap should outline a detailed implementation plan. This plan should include specific timelines, resource allocations, and key milestones. It's important to set realistic timelines that account for potential challenges and allow for flexibility. Resource allocation should consider not only financial resources but also personnel and technology requirements. Identifying key milestones helps track progress and ensures that the project remains on schedule.

Communication is a critical component of the automation roadmap. Keeping all stakeholders informed and engaged throughout the process is essential for success. Regular updates and feedback loops help identify potential issues early on and ensure that the project remains aligned with organizational goals. Transparent communication fosters a culture of collaboration and helps build trust among employees, who may have concerns about the impact of automation on their roles.

Training and support are also vital elements of the roadmap. As automation is implemented, employees may need to adapt to new technologies and processes. Providing comprehensive training and ongoing support helps ease the transition and ensures that employees are equipped to succeed in their new roles. By investing in employee development, organizations can foster a positive attitude towards automation and enhance overall productivity.

Risk management is another important consideration in the automation roadmap. Implementing automation can introduce new risks, such as system failures or data breaches. It's essential to conduct a thorough risk assessment and implement appropriate safeguards to mitigate these risks. This may involve developing contingency plans, investing in cybersecurity measures, or conducting regular audits to ensure compliance with industry standards.

Measuring success is a crucial aspect of the automation roadmap. Establishing clear metrics and KPIs allows organizations to evaluate the effectiveness of their automation efforts. These metrics should be aligned with the organization's strategic objectives and provide a comprehensive view of the impact of automation on business performance. Regular monitoring and evaluation help identify areas for improvement and ensure that automation initiatives continue to deliver value over time.

Continuous improvement is the final component of the automation roadmap. As technology evolves and business needs change, it's important to regularly review and update automation initiatives. This involves gathering feedback from employees and stakeholders, analyzing performance metrics, and making adjustments as needed. By fostering a culture of continuous improvement, organizations can ensure that their automation efforts remain relevant and effective in the long term.

Creating an automation roadmap is a complex and dynamic process that requires careful planning, collaboration, and adaptability. By conducting a thorough assessment of the current state, defining clear goals for the future state, identifying and prioritizing processes for automation, developing a detailed implementation plan, fostering communication and training, managing risks, measuring success, and embracing continuous improvement, organizations can successfully navigate the journey towards automation and achieve their strategic objectives.

Chapter 3: Essential Automation Tools

Project Management Software

Project management software has become an indispensable tool for organizations seeking to streamline their operations, enhance collaboration, and improve overall efficiency. As businesses grow and projects become more complex, the need for a centralized platform to manage tasks, resources, and timelines becomes increasingly critical. Understanding the capabilities and benefits of project management software is essential for anyone looking to optimize their project workflows.

At its core, project management software serves as a digital hub where teams can plan, execute, and monitor projects from start to finish. It provides a structured framework that helps project managers allocate resources, assign tasks, and track progress in real-time. This centralized approach not only improves visibility but also fosters accountability among team members, as everyone can see who is responsible for what and when tasks are due.

One of the primary advantages of project management software is its ability to facilitate communication and collaboration. In today's fast-paced business environment, teams are often dispersed across different locations and time zones. Project management software bridges these gaps by providing a platform where team members can communicate, share files, and collaborate on tasks seamlessly. Features such as chat functions, file sharing, and comment threads ensure that everyone stays on the same page, reducing the risk of miscommunication and errors.

Another key benefit of project management software is its ability to automate routine tasks and processes. By automating repetitive tasks such as scheduling, reminders, and status updates, project managers can free up valuable time to focus on more strategic activities. Automation also reduces the likelihood of human error, ensuring that tasks are completed accurately and on time. This increased efficiency can lead to significant cost savings and improved project outcomes.

Project management software also provides powerful tools for tracking and reporting. With built-in analytics and reporting features, project managers can gain valuable insights into project performance and identify areas for improvement. These insights can be used to make data-driven decisions, optimize resource allocation, and ensure that projects stay on track. By providing a clear picture of project progress, project management software helps organizations achieve their goals more effectively.

When selecting project management software, it's important to consider the specific needs and requirements of your organization. There are numerous options available, each with its own set of features and capabilities. Some software solutions are designed for small teams and simple projects, while others are tailored for large enterprises with complex project portfolios. Key factors to consider include ease of use, scalability, integration capabilities, and cost.

Ease of use is a critical consideration, as the software should be intuitive and user-friendly for all team members. A steep learning curve can hinder adoption and reduce the effectiveness of the software. Look for solutions that offer a clean, intuitive interface and provide training resources or customer support to assist with onboarding.

Scalability is another important factor, especially for growing organizations. The software should be able to accommodate an increasing number of users and projects without sacrificing performance. Consider whether the solution can scale with your organization and whether it offers features that support growth, such as advanced reporting and resource management tools.

Integration capabilities are also crucial, as project management software should seamlessly integrate with other tools and systems used by your organization. This includes communication platforms, file storage solutions, and other business applications. Integration ensures that data flows smoothly between systems, reducing the need for manual data entry and minimizing the risk of errors.

Cost is always a consideration, and it's important to evaluate the total cost of ownership, including subscription fees, implementation costs, and any additional expenses for training or support. While it's tempting to choose the cheapest option, it's important to consider the value that the software provides and whether it meets the needs of your organization.

Once you've selected the right project management software, it's important to implement it effectively to maximize its benefits. Start by clearly defining your project management processes and workflows, and ensure that they align with the capabilities of the software. This may involve re-evaluating existing processes and making adjustments to optimize efficiency.

Training and support are essential for successful implementation. Provide comprehensive training for all team members to ensure they understand how to use the software effectively. Encourage open communication and feedback to identify any challenges or areas for improvement. Ongoing support and training can help ensure that the software continues to deliver value over time.

Regularly review and evaluate the performance of the software to ensure it meets the evolving needs of your organization. Gather feedback from users and stakeholders to identify any areas for improvement or additional features that may be needed. By continuously optimizing your use of project management software, you can ensure that it remains a valuable asset for your organization.

Project management software is a powerful tool that can transform the way organizations manage projects. By providing a centralized platform for planning, execution, and monitoring, it enhances collaboration, improves efficiency, and drives better project outcomes. By carefully selecting and implementing the right software, organizations can unlock the full potential of their project management efforts and achieve their strategic objectives.

Email Automation Tools

Email automation tools have revolutionized the way businesses communicate with their audience, offering a streamlined approach to managing email campaigns, nurturing leads, and maintaining customer relationships. These tools are designed to automate repetitive tasks, allowing marketers to focus on crafting compelling content and strategies that drive engagement and conversions. For beginners, understanding the capabilities and benefits of email automation tools is crucial to leveraging their full potential.

At the heart of email automation lies the ability to send targeted messages to specific segments of your audience based on predefined triggers or actions. This level of personalization ensures that recipients receive relevant content that resonates with their interests and needs. By segmenting your audience and tailoring your messages accordingly, you can significantly improve open rates, click-through rates, and overall engagement.

One of the primary advantages of email automation tools is their ability to save time and resources. By automating routine tasks such as sending welcome emails, follow-up messages, and promotional offers, marketers can focus on more strategic activities that require human creativity and insight. This not only increases efficiency but also ensures consistency in communication, as automated emails are sent at the right time without the risk of human error.

Email automation tools also provide valuable insights into the performance of your campaigns. With built-in analytics and reporting features, you can track key metrics such as open rates, click-through rates, and conversion rates. These insights allow you to assess the effectiveness of your campaigns and make data-driven decisions to optimize future efforts. By understanding what works and what doesn't, you can refine your strategies and achieve better results over time.

When selecting an email automation tool, it's important to consider the specific needs and goals of your business. There are numerous options available, each with its own set of features and capabilities. Some tools are designed for small businesses with basic needs, while others offer advanced features for larger enterprises with complex marketing strategies. Key factors to consider include ease of use, integration capabilities, scalability, and cost.

Ease of use is a critical consideration, as the tool should be intuitive and user-friendly for all team members. A steep learning curve can hinder adoption and reduce the effectiveness of the tool. Look for solutions that offer a clean, intuitive interface and provide training resources or customer support to assist with onboarding.

Integration capabilities are also crucial, as email automation tools should seamlessly integrate with other tools and systems used by your organization. This includes customer relationship management (CRM) systems, e-commerce platforms, and analytics tools. Integration ensures that data flows smoothly between systems, reducing the need for manual data entry and minimizing the risk of errors.

Scalability is another important factor, especially for growing businesses. The tool should be able to accommodate an increasing number of subscribers and campaigns without sacrificing performance. Consider whether the solution can scale with your business and whether it offers features that support growth, such as advanced segmentation and personalization options.

Cost is always a consideration, and it's important to evaluate the total cost of ownership, including subscription fees, implementation costs, and any additional expenses for training or support. While it's tempting to choose the cheapest option, it's important to consider the value that the tool provides and whether it meets the needs of your business.

Once you've selected the right email automation tool, it's important to implement it effectively to maximize its benefits. Start by clearly defining your email marketing goals and strategies, and ensure that they align with the capabilities of the tool. This may involve re-evaluating existing processes and making adjustments to optimize efficiency.

Training and support are essential for successful implementation. Provide comprehensive training for all team members to ensure they understand how to use the tool effectively. Encourage open communication and feedback to identify any challenges or areas for improvement. Ongoing support and training can help ensure that the tool continues to deliver value over time.

Regularly review and evaluate the performance of your email campaigns to ensure they meet the evolving needs of your audience. Gather feedback from subscribers and stakeholders to identify any areas for improvement or additional features that may be needed. By continuously optimizing your use of email automation tools, you can ensure that they remain a valuable asset for your business.

Email automation tools are a powerful resource that can transform the way businesses communicate with their audience. By providing a streamlined approach to managing email campaigns, they enhance efficiency, improve engagement, and drive better results. By carefully selecting and implementing the right tool, businesses can unlock the full potential of their email marketing efforts and achieve their strategic objectives.

Document Management Systems

Document management systems (DMS) have become indispensable tools for organizations seeking to streamline their operations, enhance collaboration, and maintain control over their vast repositories of information. These systems offer a centralized platform for storing, organizing, and retrieving documents, enabling businesses to manage their data efficiently and securely. For beginners, understanding the core functionalities and benefits of document management systems is crucial to harnessing their full potential.

At the heart of any document management system is the ability to store and organize documents in a structured manner. This involves categorizing files based on specific criteria such as type, date, author, or project, making it easier for users to locate and access the information they need. By implementing a logical and intuitive filing system, organizations can reduce the time spent searching for documents and improve overall productivity.

One of the primary advantages of document management systems is their ability to facilitate collaboration among team members. With features such as version control, real-time editing, and commenting, DMS platforms enable multiple users to work on the same document simultaneously without the risk of overwriting each other's changes. This fosters a collaborative environment where ideas can be shared and refined, ultimately leading to better outcomes.

Security is another critical aspect of document management systems. With sensitive information often stored within these platforms, it's essential to ensure that data is protected from unauthorized access and potential breaches. DMS solutions typically offer robust security features such as encryption, access controls, and audit trails, allowing organizations to safeguard their information and comply with regulatory requirements.

Integration capabilities are also a key consideration when selecting a document management system. The ability to seamlessly integrate with other tools and systems used by the organization, such as customer relationship management (CRM) software, enterprise resource planning (ERP) systems, and email platforms, is essential for maintaining a cohesive workflow. Integration ensures that data flows smoothly between systems, reducing the need for manual data entry and minimizing the risk of errors.

Scalability is another important factor, especially for growing businesses. A document management system should be able to accommodate an increasing volume of documents and users without sacrificing performance. Consider whether the solution can scale with your business and whether it offers features that support growth, such as advanced search capabilities and customizable workflows.

When implementing a document management system, it's important to start with a clear understanding of your organization's needs and objectives. This involves assessing the current document management processes and identifying areas for improvement. By defining specific goals and requirements, you can select a DMS solution that aligns with your business needs and provides the necessary functionality.

Training and support are essential for successful implementation. Provide comprehensive training for all team members to ensure they understand how to use the system effectively. Encourage open communication and feedback to identify any challenges or areas for improvement. Ongoing support and training can help ensure that the system continues to deliver value over time.

Regularly review and evaluate the performance of your document management system to ensure it meets the evolving needs of your organization. Gather feedback from users and stakeholders to identify any areas for improvement or additional features that may be needed. By continuously optimizing your use of the DMS, you can ensure that it remains a valuable asset for your business.

Document management systems are powerful tools that can transform the way organizations manage their information. By providing a centralized platform for storing, organizing, and retrieving documents, they enhance efficiency, improve collaboration, and ensure data security. By carefully selecting and implementing the right system, businesses can unlock the full potential of their document management efforts and achieve their strategic objectives.

Customer Relationship Management (CRM) Solutions

Customer Relationship Management (CRM) solutions have become essential tools for businesses aiming to cultivate and maintain strong relationships with their customers. These systems offer a comprehensive approach to managing interactions, streamlining processes, and enhancing customer satisfaction. For beginners, understanding the core functionalities and benefits of CRM solutions is crucial to leveraging their full potential.

At the core of any CRM system is the ability to centralize customer information, providing a single source of truth for all customer-related data. This includes contact details, purchase history, communication records, and preferences. By consolidating this information, businesses can gain a holistic view of their customers, enabling them to tailor their interactions and deliver personalized experiences. This level of personalization fosters loyalty and encourages repeat business, as customers feel valued and understood.

CRM solutions also play a pivotal role in streamlining sales processes. By automating routine tasks such as lead tracking, follow-up reminders, and pipeline management, sales teams can focus on building relationships and closing deals. The system provides valuable insights into sales performance, allowing managers to identify trends, forecast revenue, and make data-driven decisions. This not only improves efficiency but also enhances the overall effectiveness of the sales team.

Marketing efforts can also benefit significantly from CRM solutions. By segmenting customers based on specific criteria such as demographics, behavior, or purchase history, businesses can create targeted marketing campaigns that resonate with their audience. CRM systems enable marketers to track the success of their campaigns, measure engagement, and refine their strategies based on real-time data. This ensures that marketing efforts are aligned with customer needs and preferences, ultimately driving better results.

Customer service is another area where CRM solutions can make a substantial impact. By providing a centralized platform for managing customer inquiries, complaints, and feedback, businesses can ensure that issues are resolved promptly and efficiently. CRM systems offer features such as ticketing, case management, and knowledge bases, enabling customer service teams to deliver consistent and high-quality support. This not only enhances customer satisfaction but also strengthens the overall brand reputation.

Integration capabilities are a key consideration when selecting a CRM solution. The ability to seamlessly integrate with other tools and systems used by the organization, such as email platforms, e-commerce systems, and social media channels, is essential for maintaining a cohesive workflow. Integration ensures that data flows smoothly between systems, reducing the need for manual data entry and minimizing the risk of errors.

Scalability is another important factor, especially for growing businesses. A CRM solution should be able to accommodate an increasing number of customers and users without sacrificing performance. Consider whether the solution can scale with your business and whether it offers features that support growth, such as advanced analytics and customizable workflows.

When implementing a CRM solution, it's important to start with a clear understanding of your organization's needs and objectives. This involves assessing the current customer relationship management processes and identifying areas for improvement. By defining specific goals and requirements, you can select a CRM solution that aligns with your business needs and provides the necessary functionality.

Training and support are essential for successful implementation. Provide comprehensive training for all team members to ensure they understand how to use the system effectively. Encourage open communication and feedback to identify any challenges or areas for improvement. Ongoing support and training can help ensure that the system continues to deliver value over time.

Regularly review and evaluate the performance of your CRM solution to ensure it meets the evolving needs of your organization. Gather feedback from users and stakeholders to identify any areas for improvement or additional features that may be needed. By continuously optimizing your use of the CRM, you can ensure that it remains a valuable asset for your business.

CRM solutions are powerful tools that can transform the way organizations manage their customer relationships. By providing a centralized platform for storing, organizing, and analyzing customer data, they enhance efficiency, improve customer satisfaction, and drive better business outcomes. By carefully selecting and implementing the right system, businesses can unlock the full potential of their customer relationship management efforts and achieve their strategic objectives.

Communication and Collaboration Platforms

Communication and collaboration platforms have revolutionized the way organizations operate, breaking down geographical barriers and enabling seamless interaction among team members. These platforms are indispensable for businesses striving to enhance productivity, foster innovation, and maintain a competitive edge in today's fast-paced environment. For beginners, understanding the functionalities and advantages of these platforms is crucial to maximizing their potential.

The essence of communication and collaboration platforms lies in their ability to connect individuals, regardless of their physical location. By providing a virtual space where team members can interact in real-time, these platforms facilitate the exchange of ideas, feedback, and information. This connectivity is particularly valuable for remote teams, as it ensures that all members remain engaged and informed, contributing to a cohesive and efficient workflow.

One of the primary features of these platforms is instant messaging, which allows for quick and direct communication between team members. Unlike traditional email, instant messaging enables real-time conversations, reducing the time spent waiting for responses and allowing for more dynamic interactions. This Immediacy is particularly beneficial for addressing urgent issues or clarifying misunderstandings, ensuring that projects stay on track and deadlines are met.

Video conferencing is another critical component of communication and collaboration platforms. By enabling face-to-face interactions, video conferencing bridges the gap between remote and in-office employees, fostering a sense of connection and camaraderie. This visual element is essential for building trust and rapport among team members, as it allows for non-verbal cues and expressions to be conveyed, enhancing the overall communication experience.

Collaboration platforms also offer tools for document sharing and co-editing, streamlining the process of working on projects collectively. By providing a centralized location for storing and accessing files, these platforms eliminate the need for cumbersome email attachments and ensure that all team members have access to the most up-to-date information. Co-editing features allow multiple users to work on the same document simultaneously, promoting collaboration and reducing the risk of version control issues.

Task management and project tracking are additional functionalities that enhance the effectiveness of communication and collaboration platforms. By providing tools for assigning tasks, setting deadlines, and monitoring progress, these platforms help teams stay organized and focused on their objectives. This level of transparency ensures that all members are aware of their responsibilities and can prioritize their work accordingly, leading to more efficient and successful project outcomes.

Integration capabilities are a key consideration when selecting a communication and collaboration platform. The ability to seamlessly integrate with other tools and systems used by the organization, such as customer relationship management (CRM) software, enterprise resource planning (ERP) systems, and email platforms, is essential for maintaining a cohesive workflow. Integration ensures that data flows smoothly between systems, reducing the need for manual data entry and minimizing the risk of errors.

Security is another critical aspect of communication and collaboration platforms. With sensitive information often shared and stored within these systems, it's essential to ensure that data is protected from unauthorized access and potential breaches. Platforms typically offer robust security features such as encryption, access controls, and audit trails, allowing organizations to safeguard their information and comply with regulatory requirements.

When implementing a communication and collaboration platform, it's important to start with a clear understanding of your organization's needs and objectives. This involves assessing the current communication and collaboration processes and identifying areas for improvement. By defining specific goals and requirements, you can select a platform that aligns with your business needs and provides the necessary functionality.

Training and support are essential for successful implementation. Provide comprehensive training for all team members to ensure they understand how to use the platform effectively. Encourage open communication and feedback to identify any challenges or areas for improvement. Ongoing support and training can help ensure that the platform continues to deliver value over time.

Regularly review and evaluate the performance of your communication and collaboration platform to ensure it meets the evolving needs of your organization. Gather feedback from users and stakeholders to identify any areas for improvement or additional features that may be needed. By continuously optimizing your use of the platform, you can ensure that it remains a valuable asset for your business.

Communication and collaboration platforms are powerful tools that can transform the way organizations operate. By providing a centralized space for interaction, information sharing, and project management, they enhance efficiency, foster innovation, and strengthen team dynamics. By carefully selecting and implementing the right platform, businesses can unlock the full potential of their communication and collaboration efforts and achieve their strategic objectives.

Chapter 4: Automating Routine Administrative Tasks

Scheduling and Calendar Management

Efficient scheduling and calendar management are vital skills for anyone looking to optimize their productivity and maintain a balanced lifestyle. In a world where time is a precious commodity, mastering these skills can make the difference between a chaotic day and a well-organized one. For beginners, understanding the principles and tools available for effective scheduling and calendar management is the first step toward achieving greater control over their time.

The foundation of successful scheduling lies in setting clear priorities. Begin by identifying the tasks and activities that are most important to you, both personally and professionally. This involves distinguishing between urgent and important tasks, a concept popularized by the Eisenhower Matrix. Urgent tasks require immediate attention, while important tasks contribute to long-term goals and values. By categorizing tasks in this way, you can allocate your time more effectively, ensuring that you focus on what truly matters.

Once priorities are established, it's essential to create a structured schedule that reflects these priorities. Start by blocking out time for high-priority tasks, ensuring that you allocate sufficient time to complete them without feeling rushed. Consider your natural energy levels and productivity patterns when scheduling tasks. For instance, if you're most alert and focused in the morning, reserve this time for tasks that require deep concentration and critical thinking.

Incorporating buffer time into your schedule is another crucial aspect of effective calendar management. Buffer time acts as a cushion between tasks, allowing for unexpected delays or interruptions. This flexibility reduces stress and prevents the domino effect of one delayed task impacting the rest of your day. By building in buffer time, you can maintain a more relaxed and adaptable approach to your schedule.

Digital calendar tools have become indispensable for managing schedules efficiently. These tools offer features such as reminders, recurring events, and color-coded categories, making it easier to organize and visualize your commitments. Popular digital calendars like Google Calendar and Microsoft Outlook allow for seamless integration with other productivity tools, enabling you to synchronize tasks, appointments, and deadlines across platforms.

When using digital calendars, take advantage of the ability to set reminders and notifications. These features help ensure that you don't overlook important tasks or appointments. Customize notifications to suit your preferences, whether it's a gentle nudge a day before a meeting or a more immediate alert an hour prior. By tailoring reminders to your needs, you can stay on top of your schedule without feeling overwhelmed.

Sharing your calendar with colleagues, family members, or friends can enhance collaboration and communication. By granting access to your calendar, others can view your availability and schedule meetings or events accordingly. This transparency reduces the back-and-forth communication often required to coordinate schedules, saving time and minimizing misunderstandings.

While digital tools offer numerous advantages, some individuals may prefer the tactile experience of a physical planner. A paper planner can provide a sense of satisfaction and mindfulness that digital tools may lack. Writing tasks and appointments by hand can reinforce memory and encourage reflection on your priorities. If you choose to use a paper planner, consider incorporating elements such as daily to-do lists, weekly goals, and monthly overviews to maintain a comprehensive view of your schedule.

Time blocking is a powerful technique that can enhance your scheduling and calendar management efforts. By dedicating specific blocks of time to particular tasks or activities, you create a focused environment that minimizes distractions and increases productivity. Time blocking encourages you to commit to tasks fully, reducing the temptation to multitask or procrastinate. Experiment with different time block durations to find what works best for you, whether it's 25-minute Pomodoro sessions or longer, uninterrupted work periods.

Regularly reviewing and adjusting your schedule is essential for maintaining its effectiveness. Set aside time each week to reflect on your accomplishments and assess whether your schedule aligns with your priorities. Identify any patterns or recurring challenges that may be hindering your productivity, and make necessary adjustments to address these issues. This ongoing evaluation ensures that your schedule remains dynamic and responsive to your evolving needs.

Incorporating self-care and downtime into your schedule is equally important. While it's tempting to fill every available moment with tasks and commitments, neglecting self-care can lead to burnout and decreased productivity. Schedule regular breaks, exercise, and leisure activities to recharge your energy and maintain a healthy work-life balance. By prioritizing self-care, you can sustain your productivity and well-being over the long term.

Effective scheduling and calendar management require a combination of strategic planning, the right tools, and a commitment to continuous improvement. By setting clear priorities, utilizing digital or physical tools, and regularly reviewing your schedule, you can take control of your time and achieve your goals with greater ease. Whether you're managing a busy work schedule, balancing personal commitments, or pursuing new opportunities, mastering these skills will empower you to navigate the complexities of modern life with confidence and clarity.

Expense Tracking and Reporting

Managing personal finances can often feel like navigating a labyrinth, with expenses lurking around every corner. Expense tracking and reporting serve as the guiding light through this maze, offering clarity and control over one's financial landscape. For beginners, mastering these skills is crucial for building a solid financial foundation and achieving long-term financial goals.

The journey begins with understanding the importance of tracking expenses. By keeping a detailed record of every transaction, you gain insight into your spending habits and patterns. This awareness is the first step toward making informed financial decisions. It allows you to identify areas where you may be overspending and helps you allocate resources more effectively. Tracking expenses also provides a clear picture of your cash flow, ensuring that you live within your means and avoid unnecessary debt.

To start tracking expenses, choose a method that suits your lifestyle and preferences. Some individuals prefer the simplicity of pen and paper, jotting down each expense in a dedicated notebook. Others may opt for digital solutions, such as spreadsheets or mobile apps, which offer the convenience of automation and real-time updates. Whichever method you choose, consistency is key. Make it a habit to record expenses as they occur, rather than relying on memory at the end of the week or month.

Categorizing expenses is an essential aspect of effective tracking. By grouping similar expenses together, you can better understand where your money is going and identify potential areas for adjustment. Common categories include housing, transportation, groceries, dining out, entertainment, and savings. Tailor these categories to fit your unique financial situation, adding or removing categories as needed. This customization ensures that your expense tracking system reflects your personal priorities and goals.

Once expenses are categorized, it's time to analyze the data. Review your spending patterns regularly, whether it's weekly, monthly, or quarterly. Look for trends and anomalies that may indicate a need for change. For instance, if dining out expenses consistently exceed your budget, consider cooking more meals at home or exploring budget-friendly dining options. By analyzing your spending habits, you can make proactive adjustments that align with your financial objectives.

Expense reporting takes tracking to the next level by providing a comprehensive overview of your financial situation. Reports can be generated manually or through digital tools, offering a snapshot of your income, expenses, and savings over a specific period. These reports serve as valuable tools for budgeting, financial planning, and decision-making. They allow you to assess your progress toward financial goals and make informed adjustments as needed.

Creating an expense report involves compiling data from your tracking system and organizing it into a clear and concise format. Start by listing all sources of income, followed by a detailed breakdown of expenses by category. Include any savings or investments, as well as outstanding debts or liabilities. This comprehensive view of your finances provides a foundation for setting realistic budgets and financial goals.

Budgeting is a natural extension of expense tracking and reporting. With a clear understanding of your financial situation, you can create a budget that reflects your priorities and constraints. Begin by setting specific, measurable goals, such as saving for a vacation, paying off debt, or building an emergency fund. Allocate funds to each category based on your goals and past spending patterns, ensuring that your budget is both realistic and achievable.

As you implement your budget, continue to track expenses and generate reports to monitor your progress. Regularly compare your actual spending to your budgeted amounts, identifying any discrepancies or areas for improvement. This ongoing evaluation allows you to make necessary adjustments and stay on track toward your financial goals.

In addition to personal finance management, expense tracking and reporting are essential skills in a professional context. For business owners and employees, accurate expense tracking is crucial for maintaining financial transparency and accountability. It ensures that business expenses are properly documented and reimbursed, and it provides valuable data for financial analysis and decision-making.

In a business setting, expense reports often require additional documentation, such as receipts or invoices, to verify the legitimacy of expenses. Implementing a standardized process for submitting and reviewing expense reports can streamline this process and reduce the risk of errors or discrepancies. Digital tools and software can further enhance efficiency by automating data entry and report generation.

Whether for personal or professional purposes, effective expense tracking and reporting require discipline, attention to detail, and a commitment to continuous improvement. By developing these skills, you gain greater control over your finances and empower yourself to make informed decisions that support your long-term goals. As you navigate the complexities of modern life, let expense tracking and reporting be your compass, guiding you toward financial stability and success.

Invoicing and Billing Automation

In the bustling world of business, time is a precious commodity. Every minute spent on administrative tasks is a minute taken away from strategic planning and growth. Invoicing and billing, though essential, can often become time-consuming and error-prone when handled manually. Automation emerges as a powerful ally, streamlining these processes and freeing up valuable resources for more critical endeavors.

The first step in embracing invoicing and billing automation is understanding its benefits. Automation reduces the likelihood of human error, ensuring that invoices are accurate and consistent. This accuracy not only enhances the professionalism of your business but also minimizes disputes and delays in payment. Moreover, automated systems can handle large volumes of invoices with ease, allowing businesses to scale operations without a corresponding increase in administrative workload.

Choosing the right invoicing and billing software is crucial for successful automation. With a plethora of options available, it's important to select a solution that aligns with your business needs and integrates seamlessly with existing systems. Consider factors such as ease of use, customization options, and customer support when evaluating potential software. A user-friendly interface ensures that your team can quickly adapt to the new system, while customization allows you to tailor invoices to reflect your brand identity.

Once the software is in place, setting up automated invoicing involves configuring templates and schedules. Templates provide a standardized format for invoices, ensuring consistency across all transactions. They can be customized to include essential details such as payment terms, due dates, and contact information. Automated scheduling allows invoices to be generated and sent at predetermined intervals, reducing the risk of missed or late invoices. This regularity not only improves cash flow but also fosters trust and reliability with clients.

Automation also extends to payment processing, offering clients a seamless and convenient experience. By integrating payment gateways with your invoicing system, clients can settle invoices with just a few clicks. This convenience encourages prompt payment and reduces the administrative burden of tracking and reconciling payments. Additionally, automated reminders can be set up to notify clients of upcoming due dates or overdue invoices, further enhancing the efficiency of the billing process.

Data security is a paramount concern when automating invoicing and billing. Sensitive financial information must be protected from unauthorized access and breaches. Ensure that your chosen software complies with industry standards and regulations, such as GDPR or PCI-DSS, to safeguard client data. Regularly update software and implement robust security measures, such as encryption and two-factor authentication, to maintain the integrity of your invoicing system.

The transition to automated invoicing and billing may require a shift in mindset and processes. Training and support are essential to ensure that your team is equipped to leverage the full potential of the new system. Provide comprehensive training sessions and resources to familiarize employees with the software's features and functionalities. Encourage open communication and feedback to address any challenges or concerns that may arise during the transition.

As your business grows, automated invoicing and billing systems can adapt to changing needs and demands. Scalability is a key advantage of automation, allowing you to handle increased transaction volumes without compromising efficiency or accuracy. Regularly review and assess your invoicing processes to identify opportunities for further optimization and improvement.

This proactive approach ensures that your business remains agile and responsive in a dynamic market environment.

Invoicing and billing automation is not just a tool for efficiency; it is a strategic asset that can drive business growth and success. By streamlining administrative tasks, businesses can focus on delivering exceptional value to clients and pursuing new opportunities. The time and resources saved through automation can be reinvested in innovation, customer service, and strategic initiatives, propelling your business toward its goals.

In the ever-evolving landscape of business, staying ahead of the curve requires embracing technology and innovation. Invoicing and billing automation is a testament to the transformative power of technology, offering businesses a competitive edge in a fast-paced world. By harnessing the capabilities of automation, businesses can achieve greater efficiency, accuracy, and scalability, paving the way for sustained growth and success.

Data Entry and Database Management

Data entry and database management form the backbone of any organization, serving as the foundation upon which critical decisions are made. The accuracy and efficiency of these processes can significantly impact a business's operations, making it essential to understand and implement best practices.

Data entry, at its core, involves the input of information into a system. This seemingly simple task requires precision and attention to detail, as errors can lead to costly mistakes and misinformed decisions. To ensure accuracy, it's crucial to establish a standardized process for data entry. This includes creating clear guidelines for data formatting, validation, and verification. Consistency in data entry not only minimizes errors but also facilitates easier data retrieval and analysis.

Training is a vital component in maintaining high standards of data entry. Employees responsible for this task should be well-versed in the tools and software they use, as well as the specific requirements of the data they handle. Regular training sessions and workshops can help keep skills sharp and introduce new techniques or technologies that enhance efficiency. Encouraging a culture of continuous learning and improvement can lead to more accurate and reliable data entry practices.

Database management, on the other hand, involves organizing, storing, and retrieving data in a way that maximizes its utility. A well-managed database is a powerful tool, enabling businesses to access and analyze information quickly and effectively. The first step in effective database management is selecting the right database system. Factors to consider include the size and complexity of the data, the level of security required, and the ease of integration with existing systems. Popular database management systems include SQL, Oracle, and MongoDB, each offering unique features and capabilities.

Once a database system is in place, structuring the data efficiently is paramount. This involves designing a logical schema that organizes data into tables, fields, and relationships. A well-structured database not only improves data retrieval speed but also enhances data integrity and reduces redundancy. Normalization is a key technique in database design, ensuring that data is stored in a way that minimizes duplication and maintains consistency.

Data security is a critical aspect of database management, as databases often contain sensitive and confidential information. Implementing robust security measures, such as encryption, access controls, and regular audits, can protect data from unauthorized access and breaches. It's also important to establish a data backup and recovery plan to safeguard against data loss due to hardware failures, cyberattacks, or natural disasters. Regularly testing and updating these security protocols ensures that they remain effective in an ever-evolving threat landscape.

Database management also involves maintaining data quality and integrity. This requires regular data cleaning and validation processes to identify and correct errors, inconsistencies, or outdated information. Data quality metrics, such as accuracy, completeness, and timeliness, can be used to assess and improve the overall quality of the data. Implementing automated data validation tools can streamline this process, reducing the manual effort required and increasing the reliability of the data.

As businesses grow and evolve, their data needs may change, necessitating adjustments to the database structure or management practices. Scalability is an important consideration in database management, ensuring that the system can accommodate increasing volumes of data without compromising performance. Regularly reviewing and optimizing database performance can help identify bottlenecks or inefficiencies, allowing for timely interventions and improvements.

Effective data entry and database management are not just about technology; they also involve people and processes. Fostering a culture of data stewardship, where employees understand the importance of data accuracy and integrity, can lead to more responsible data handling practices. Encouraging collaboration and communication between departments can also enhance data management efforts, ensuring that data is used effectively across the organization.

In the digital age, data is a valuable asset that can drive innovation, inform strategy, and create competitive advantages. By mastering data entry and database management, businesses can unlock the full potential of their data, transforming it into actionable insights and informed decisions. The journey to effective data management is ongoing, requiring continuous learning, adaptation, and improvement. However, the rewards of a well-managed data system are immense, offering businesses the clarity and confidence to navigate an increasingly complex and data-driven world.

HR Processes and Recruitment Automation

Navigating the intricate world of human resources (HR) requires a blend of strategic insight and operational efficiency. As organizations strive to attract and retain top talent, the role of HR processes and recruitment automation becomes increasingly pivotal. These elements not only streamline operations but also enhance the candidate experience, ultimately contributing to a more dynamic and responsive workforce.

HR processes encompass a wide range of activities, from onboarding and performance management to employee engagement and compliance. At the heart of these processes lies the need for consistency and transparency. Establishing clear policies and procedures ensures that all employees are treated fairly and equitably, fostering a culture of trust and respect. This foundation is crucial for building a positive organizational culture, where employees feel valued and motivated to contribute their best efforts.

Recruitment, a critical component of HR, has undergone a significant transformation with the advent of automation technologies. Traditional recruitment methods, often characterized by manual and time-consuming tasks, are being replaced by automated solutions that offer speed and precision. Recruitment automation leverages technology to streamline various stages of the hiring process, from sourcing and screening candidates to scheduling interviews and extending offers.

One of the primary benefits of recruitment automation is its ability to enhance efficiency. Automated systems can quickly sift through large volumes of applications, identifying the most qualified candidates based on predefined criteria. This not only reduces the time-to-hire but also allows HR professionals to focus on more strategic activities, such as building relationships with potential hires and developing talent pipelines.

Moreover, recruitment automation can significantly improve the candidate experience. By providing timely and personalized communication, automated systems keep candidates informed and engaged throughout the hiring process. This level of responsiveness can set an organization apart in a competitive job market, where candidates often have multiple options to consider. A positive candidate experience not only increases the likelihood of securing top talent but also enhances the organization's reputation as an employer of choice.

Data-driven decision-making is another advantage of recruitment automation. By collecting and analyzing data at each stage of the hiring process, organizations can gain valuable insights into their recruitment strategies and identify areas for improvement. Metrics such as time-to-fill, cost-per-hire, and candidate satisfaction can inform strategic decisions and drive continuous improvement. This data-centric approach ensures that recruitment efforts are aligned with organizational goals and contribute to long-term success.

Despite the numerous benefits, the implementation of recruitment automation requires careful consideration and planning. Organizations must select the right tools and technologies that align with their specific needs and objectives. Factors such as scalability, integration capabilities, and user-friendliness should be taken into account when evaluating potential solutions. Additionally, it's essential to ensure that automated systems comply with relevant regulations and standards, such as data privacy and equal employment opportunity laws.

Training and change management are critical components of successful recruitment automation. HR professionals must be equipped with the skills and knowledge to effectively utilize automated systems and interpret the data they generate. Providing comprehensive training and support can facilitate a smooth transition and maximize the benefits of automation. Moreover, fostering a culture of adaptability and innovation can help employees embrace new technologies and processes, driving organizational growth and success.

While recruitment automation offers numerous advantages, it's important to recognize that it cannot replace the human touch. Building meaningful relationships with candidates and understanding their unique needs and aspirations remain essential aspects of the recruitment process. Automation should be viewed as a tool that enhances, rather than replaces, the human element of HR. By striking the right balance between technology and human interaction, organizations can create a recruitment process that is both efficient and empathetic.

As the HR landscape continues to evolve, the integration of automation technologies will play an increasingly important role in shaping the future of work. By embracing these innovations, organizations can not only improve their recruitment processes but also create a more agile and resilient workforce. The journey towards recruitment automation is one of continuous learning and adaptation, requiring organizations to stay abreast of emerging trends and technologies. However, the rewards of a well-executed automation strategy are substantial, offering organizations the opportunity to attract and retain the talent they need to thrive in a rapidly changing world.

Chapter 5: Enhancing Communication and Collaboration

Automated Email Campaigns

Crafting an effective automated email campaign is akin to orchestrating a symphony, where each note must resonate with precision and purpose. In the digital age, email remains a powerful tool for communication, marketing, and engagement. However, the sheer volume of emails that flood inboxes daily necessitates a strategic approach to ensure that your message not only reaches its intended audience but also captures their attention and prompts action.

The foundation of a successful automated email campaign lies in understanding your audience. This involves segmenting your email list based on various criteria such as demographics, behavior, and preferences. By tailoring your messages to specific segments, you can deliver content that is relevant and personalized, increasing the likelihood of engagement. For instance, a clothing retailer might segment their list by gender, purchase history, or geographic location, allowing them to send targeted promotions that resonate with each group.

Once you have a clear understanding of your audience, the next step is to define the goals of your campaign. Are you aiming to drive sales, increase website traffic, or nurture leads? Having a clear objective will guide the content and structure of your emails, ensuring that each message aligns with your overarching strategy. It's important to set measurable goals, such as a specific increase in click-through rates or a target number of conversions, to evaluate the success of your campaign.

Crafting compelling content is at the heart of any email campaign. The subject line serves as the first impression, and it must be both intriguing and informative to entice recipients to open the email. A well-crafted subject line can significantly impact open rates, so it's worth investing time in testing different variations to see what resonates with your audience. Once the email is opened, the content should be concise, engaging, and aligned with the recipient's interests. Incorporating storytelling elements can make your message more relatable and memorable, while a clear call-to-action (CTA) directs recipients towards the desired outcome.

Automation technology allows you to schedule and send emails at optimal times, ensuring that your message reaches recipients when they are most likely to engage. This can be particularly effective for nurturing leads, where a series of automated emails guide prospects through the sales funnel. For example, a software company might send a sequence of emails that introduce the product, share customer testimonials, and offer a free trial, gradually building trust and encouraging conversion.

Personalization is a key component of automated email campaigns. By leveraging data such as the recipient's name, past interactions, and purchase history, you can create emails that feel tailored to the individual. This level of personalization can significantly enhance engagement, as recipients are more likely to respond to messages that speak directly to their needs and preferences. Dynamic content, which changes based on the recipient's characteristics, can further enhance personalization by delivering relevant offers or recommendations.

Testing and optimization are crucial for maximizing the effectiveness of your email campaigns. A/B testing allows you to experiment with different elements of your emails, such as subject lines, content, and CTAs, to determine what resonates best with your audience. By analyzing the results, you can make data-driven decisions to refine your strategy and improve performance. Additionally, monitoring key metrics such as open rates, click-through rates, and conversion rates provides valuable insights into the success of your campaign and areas for improvement.

Compliance with regulations such as the General Data Protection Regulation (GDPR) and the CAN-SPAM Act is essential for maintaining trust and avoiding legal repercussions. This involves obtaining explicit consent from recipients to receive emails, providing clear opt-out options, and ensuring that your emails are truthful and not misleading. By adhering to these regulations, you demonstrate respect for your audience's privacy and build a foundation of trust.

The integration of automated email campaigns with other marketing channels can amplify their impact. For instance, combining email with social media or content marketing can create a cohesive and multi-faceted strategy that reaches your audience through multiple touchpoints. This integrated approach not only reinforces your message but also provides a more comprehensive view of your audience's behavior and preferences, enabling you to deliver even more targeted and effective campaigns.

In the ever-evolving landscape of digital marketing, staying abreast of emerging trends and technologies is crucial for maintaining a competitive edge. Innovations such as artificial intelligence and machine learning are transforming the way email campaigns are designed and executed, offering new opportunities for personalization and optimization. By embracing these advancements, you can enhance the effectiveness of your campaigns and deliver a more engaging and relevant experience for your audience.

Ultimately, the success of an automated email campaign hinges on its ability to connect with recipients on a personal level, delivering value and fostering a sense of trust and loyalty. By combining strategic planning, compelling content, and cutting-edge technology, you can create campaigns that not only achieve your goals but also resonate with your audience, driving long-term success and growth.

Chatbots for Internal and External Communication

Chatbots have emerged as a transformative tool in the realm of communication, offering businesses a versatile solution for both internal and external interactions. Their ability to streamline processes, enhance customer engagement, and facilitate seamless communication makes them an invaluable asset in today's fast-paced digital landscape. Understanding how to effectively implement chatbots for communication requires a nuanced approach that considers the unique needs of both internal teams and external audiences.

Internally, chatbots can revolutionize the way organizations manage their operations. By automating routine tasks and providing instant access to information, chatbots free up valuable time for employees to focus on more strategic initiatives. For instance, a human resources department can deploy a chatbot to handle common inquiries about company policies, benefits, or leave requests. This not only reduces the workload on HR staff but also ensures that employees receive accurate and timely information. Additionally, chatbots can assist in onboarding new employees by guiding them through the necessary paperwork and training modules, creating a more efficient and welcoming experience.

In the realm of project management, chatbots can serve as virtual assistants, helping teams stay organized and on track. They can send reminders about upcoming deadlines, provide updates on project status, and facilitate communication between team members. By integrating with project management tools, chatbots can pull data from various sources and present it in a cohesive manner, enabling teams to make informed decisions quickly. This level of automation and integration fosters a more collaborative and productive work environment.

Externally, chatbots play a crucial role in enhancing customer service and engagement. They provide businesses with the ability to offer 24/7 support, ensuring that customers receive assistance whenever they need it. By handling common queries and issues, chatbots reduce the burden on customer service representatives, allowing them to focus on more complex or high-priority cases. This not only improves response times but also enhances the overall customer experience.

The key to successful external communication through chatbots lies in their design and functionality. A well-designed chatbot should be intuitive, user-friendly, and capable of understanding and responding to a wide range of customer inquiries. Natural language processing (NLP) is a critical component in achieving this, as it enables chatbots to interpret and respond to human language in a way that feels natural and conversational. By continuously learning from interactions, chatbots can improve their accuracy and effectiveness over time, providing a more personalized experience for users.

Moreover, chatbots can be integrated into various communication channels, such as websites, social media platforms, and messaging apps, to reach customers where they are most active. This omnichannel approach ensures that businesses can engage with their audience across multiple touchpoints, creating a seamless and consistent experience. For example, a retail company might use a chatbot on its website to assist with product inquiries, while also deploying a chatbot on social media to handle customer feedback and support requests.

To maximize the potential of chatbots for communication, businesses must prioritize data security and privacy. As chatbots handle sensitive information, it is essential to implement robust security measures to protect user data and maintain trust. This includes encrypting data transmissions, regularly updating security protocols, and ensuring compliance with relevant regulations. By demonstrating a commitment to data protection, businesses can build confidence with both internal users and external customers.

The implementation of chatbots also requires careful planning and strategy. Businesses must identify the specific communication needs they aim to address and tailor their chatbot solutions accordingly. This involves defining clear objectives, selecting the appropriate technology, and designing a user experience that aligns with the brand's voice and values. Additionally, businesses should continuously monitor and evaluate the performance of their chatbots, using analytics and feedback to make improvements and optimize their effectiveness.

Training and support are vital components of a successful chatbot strategy. Employees must be equipped with the knowledge and skills to effectively utilize chatbots in their daily tasks, while customers should be provided with guidance on how to interact with chatbots for optimal results. By fostering a culture of learning and adaptation, businesses can ensure that their chatbot initiatives remain relevant and impactful.

The future of chatbots in communication is promising, with advancements in technology paving the way for even more sophisticated and capable solutions. As artificial intelligence and machine learning continue to evolve, chatbots will become increasingly adept at understanding and responding to complex queries, offering a level of service that rivals human interaction. This presents exciting opportunities for businesses to further enhance their communication strategies and deliver exceptional experiences for both internal teams and external audiences.

In conclusion, chatbots represent a powerful tool for transforming communication within and outside of organizations. By leveraging their capabilities, businesses can streamline operations, improve customer engagement, and foster a more connected and efficient environment. As technology continues to advance, the potential for chatbots to revolutionize communication will only grow, making them an essential component of any forward-thinking business strategy.

Video Conferencing Tools

Video conferencing tools have become indispensable in today's interconnected world, bridging geographical divides and enabling seamless communication across distances. As businesses and individuals increasingly rely on virtual interactions, understanding the nuances of these tools is crucial for effective communication and collaboration. This chapter delves into the practical aspects of video conferencing tools, offering insights and guidance for beginners seeking to harness their full potential.

The rise of video conferencing tools can be attributed to their ability to replicate face-to-face interactions, fostering a sense of presence and engagement that traditional communication methods often lack. Whether it's a business meeting, a virtual classroom, or a family gathering, these tools provide a platform for real-time interaction, complete with visual and auditory cues that enhance understanding and connection. For beginners, the first step in mastering video conferencing is selecting the right tool that aligns with their specific needs and objectives.

Several factors should be considered when choosing a video conferencing tool. Compatibility with existing devices and operating systems is paramount, as it ensures a smooth and hassle-free experience. Additionally, the tool's user interface should be intuitive and easy to navigate, minimizing the learning curve for new users. Features such as screen sharing, recording capabilities, and chat functions can significantly enhance the utility of a video conferencing tool, making it more versatile and adaptable to various scenarios.

Once a suitable tool has been selected, setting up a video conference involves several key steps. Ensuring a stable internet connection is essential, as it directly impacts the quality of the video and audio. Participants should test their microphones and cameras beforehand to avoid technical glitches during the call. Proper lighting and a clutter-free background contribute to a professional appearance, while minimizing distractions for both the speaker and the audience.

Etiquette plays a vital role in the success of a video conference. Participants should join the call on time, mute their microphones when not speaking, and use the chat function for questions or comments to avoid interrupting the flow of conversation. Maintaining eye contact by looking at the camera, rather than the screen, helps create a more engaging and personable interaction. Additionally, dressing appropriately and being mindful of body language can enhance the overall impression and effectiveness of the communication.

For businesses, video conferencing tools offer a cost-effective solution for conducting meetings, training sessions, and presentations. They eliminate the need for travel, reducing expenses and environmental impact while saving time. By facilitating remote work and collaboration, these tools enable organizations to tap into a global talent pool, fostering diversity and innovation. However, to maximize the benefits of video conferencing, businesses must establish clear protocols and guidelines for their use.

Security and privacy are critical considerations when using video conferencing tools, particularly for sensitive or confidential discussions. Users should ensure that the tool they choose offers robust encryption and security features, such as password protection and waiting rooms, to prevent unauthorized access. Regularly updating software and being vigilant about phishing attempts can further safeguard against potential threats.

In educational settings, video conferencing tools have transformed the way knowledge is imparted and received. They enable educators to reach students in remote locations, offering a flexible and accessible learning experience. Interactive features, such as breakout rooms and polls, can enhance student engagement and participation, creating a dynamic and collaborative virtual classroom. For educators, mastering these tools involves not only technical proficiency but also the ability to adapt teaching methods to suit the virtual environment.

The social aspect of video conferencing should not be overlooked. These tools provide a platform for maintaining personal connections, allowing friends and family to stay in touch despite physical distances. Virtual gatherings, celebrations, and even game nights can be organized through video conferencing, offering a sense of togetherness and community. For individuals new to video conferencing, exploring these social applications can be a fun and rewarding way to become familiar with the technology.

As video conferencing tools continue to evolve, they are likely to incorporate more advanced features and capabilities, further enhancing their utility and appeal. Artificial intelligence, virtual reality, and augmented reality are poised to play a significant role in shaping the future of video conferencing, offering new possibilities for interaction and collaboration. For beginners, staying informed about these developments and being open to experimentation can lead to a more enriching and effective video conferencing experience.

In summary, video conferencing tools have revolutionized the way we communicate, offering a versatile and powerful solution for both professional and personal interactions. By understanding the key aspects of these tools and adopting best practices, beginners can unlock their full potential and enjoy the myriad benefits they offer. As technology continues to advance, video conferencing will undoubtedly remain a cornerstone of modern communication, connecting people and ideas across the globe.

Collaborative Workspaces

Collaborative workspaces have emerged as a transformative force in the modern work environment, reshaping how teams interact, innovate, and achieve their goals. These dynamic spaces, both physical and virtual, are designed to foster creativity, enhance productivity, and facilitate seamless communication among team members. For beginners venturing into the realm of collaborative workspaces, understanding their potential and effectively utilizing them can lead to significant improvements in team performance and satisfaction.

The concept of collaborative workspaces is rooted in the idea of breaking down traditional barriers that often hinder communication and collaboration. In a physical sense, these spaces are characterized by open layouts, flexible seating arrangements, and shared resources that encourage spontaneous interactions and idea sharing. The absence of cubicles and closed offices creates an environment where team members can easily engage with one another, fostering a sense of community and collective purpose.

Virtual collaborative workspaces, on the other hand, leverage technology to connect team members across different locations and time zones. These platforms offer a suite of tools and features that facilitate real-time communication, document sharing, and project management. For beginners, selecting the right virtual workspace involves assessing the specific needs of the team and ensuring compatibility with existing systems and workflows. Key features to consider include video conferencing, instant messaging, file storage, and task tracking capabilities.

The success of a collaborative workspace hinges on the culture and mindset of the team. Encouraging open communication, mutual respect, and a willingness to share ideas are essential components of a thriving collaborative environment. Leaders play a crucial role in setting the tone, modeling collaborative behaviors, and providing the necessary support and resources for team members to succeed. By fostering a culture of trust and inclusivity, teams can unlock the full potential of their collaborative workspace.

One of the primary benefits of collaborative workspaces is their ability to enhance creativity and innovation. By bringing together diverse perspectives and expertise, these spaces create opportunities for cross-pollination of ideas and the development of novel solutions. Brainstorming sessions, workshops, and hackathons are common activities within collaborative workspaces, designed to stimulate creative thinking and problem-solving. For beginners, participating in these activities can be an invaluable learning experience, offering insights into different approaches and methodologies.

Productivity is another key advantage of collaborative workspaces. The ability to quickly access information, collaborate on documents, and communicate with team members reduces the time spent on administrative tasks and streamlines workflows. Virtual workspaces, in particular, offer the flexibility to work from anywhere, enabling teams to maintain productivity even when members are remote or traveling. For beginners, mastering the tools and features of a virtual workspace can lead to more efficient and effective work processes.

While collaborative workspaces offer numerous benefits, they also present certain challenges that teams must navigate. Distractions and noise levels in open-plan offices can hinder concentration and focus, requiring strategies to manage these potential disruptions. Virtual workspaces, meanwhile, may suffer from issues related to technology, such as connectivity problems or software glitches. Establishing clear protocols and guidelines for communication and collaboration can help mitigate these challenges and ensure a smooth and productive experience.

The role of technology in collaborative workspaces cannot be overstated. From cloud-based storage solutions to project management software, technology provides the infrastructure that supports collaboration and enables teams to work together seamlessly. For beginners, staying informed about the latest technological advancements and being open to experimentation can lead to more effective use of collaborative tools and platforms.

In addition to technology, the physical design of a collaborative workspace plays a significant role in its success. Ergonomic furniture, ample natural light, and access to amenities such as breakout areas and quiet zones contribute to a comfortable and conducive work environment. Personalization and flexibility are key considerations, allowing team members to adapt the space to suit their individual preferences and needs.

As organizations continue to embrace collaborative workspaces, the importance of continuous learning and adaptation becomes evident. Teams must be willing to experiment with different approaches, gather feedback, and make adjustments to optimize their collaborative efforts. For beginners, this process of iteration and improvement is an opportunity to develop valuable skills and insights that can be applied to future projects and endeavors.

Collaborative workspaces represent a paradigm shift in the way we work, offering a powerful framework for achieving collective success. By understanding the principles and practices that underpin these spaces, beginners can harness their potential to drive innovation, enhance productivity, and build strong, cohesive teams. As the landscape of work continues to evolve, collaborative workspaces will remain a vital component of the modern workplace, shaping the future of collaboration and teamwork.